IKEA's real Swedish food book

IKEA's real Swedish food book

Conversion table

Standard European measurements are used throughout. In case you are more familiar with Imperial or US measurements, here is a conversion table.

Imperial and American weights

1 LB = 16 OZ = 435 G
1 OZ = 28.35 G

American liquid measures

1 CUP = 2.4 DL
1 CUP = 8 FLUID OZ = 16 TABLESPOONS
1 TABLESPOON = 1.47 ML (ABOUT 1.5 ML)

Imperial liquid measures

1 CUP = 2.8 DL
1 CUP = 10 FLUID OZ = 20 TABLESPOONS
1 TABLESPOON = 1.47 ML (ABOUT 1.5 ML)

200°C = 392° F
250°C = 482° F
300°C = 572° F

ALL PHOTOGRAPHS ARE BY GUNNAR MAGNUSSON, MAGNUSSON PRODUKTION AB, MALMÖ, SWEDEN, EXCEPT FOR THE PICTURE ON PAGE 9 (TOP LEFT), WHICH IS BY KATE KÄRRBERG, THE LARGE PICTURE ON PAGE 12, WHICH IS BY BERIT DJUSE, THE PICTURES ON 10 AND 13, BY DICK CLEVESTAM, AND THE PICTURE ON PAGE 15, BY TERO NIEMI.
THE PICTURES ON PAGES 9 (TOP RIGHT), 12 (BOTTOM RIGHT), 13 (TOP LEFT), 14 AND 15 (BOTTOM LEFT) ARE THE PROPERTY OF INTER IKEA SYSTEMS.
PROJECT MANAGEMENT: LILL FORSMAN, BOKBOLAGET AB, MALMÖ, SWEDEN
DESIGN: LEIF ZIMMER, ZIMMER AB, MALMÖ, SWEDEN
EDITOR: LEIF ERIKSSON, AB ENZO D, MALMÖ, SWEDEN
RECIPES COMPOSED BY: LENNARTH BREWITZ, IKEA FOOD SERVICES, IKEA INTERNATIONAL A/S
ENGLISH TRANSLATION: ROGER TANNER, ORDVÄXLINGEN AB, SWEDEN
REPRO: PRE PRESS CENTER, LUND, SWEDEN
PRINTED BY: FÄLTH & HÄSSLER, VÄRNAMO, SWEDEN 2000, 2001, 2003
BOUND BY: FÄLTH & HÄSSLER, FARSTA, SWEDEN 2000, 2001, 2003
PAPER, INLAY: SILVERSILK 130 G
ISBN 91-7843-154-9 BOKBOLAGET

Contents

Chance to discover!

This is a book about food – the Swedish food which IKEA brings to practically every corner of the world.

Open it up, and take a look at a new, exciting culinary tradition which you can take home as your own. For a while, at least. All the recipes are based on ingredients available from the IKEA Swedish Food Market, plus others obtainable in your ordinary food store.

Bon appétit!

Needless to say, we have more than just the ingredients for the food: we can supply you with the whole party. All pots and pans, services, glassware and cutlery come from our stock range. Inspiration is just around the corner.

A bit of history

Sweden's culinary tradition, like that of any other country, springs from its history – from the northward migration of the first Swedes as they trailed the retreating ice cap, to the multi-cultural society of today, the Swedish cuisine has evolved into what is now commonly acknowledged as one of the world's most innovative.

But in this book you will look in vain for prize-winning recipes from the chef tournaments. Instead what you will find is some of the firmest favourites of Swedish home cooking.

And we don't just give you the recipes. We give you hints on how to combine and vary them, and we also tell you something of their cultural setting, which includes five of the year's main festivals.

Easter witch

Easter

Sweden is in many ways a secularised country, but any number of the traditional religious festivals live on. Easter is among the most popular, partly because – in the south of Sweden, at least – spring has begun moving into summer, with daffodils, white anemones and the first leaves on the birch trees as hopeful signs of warmer times to follow.

Easter has become one of the big Swedish culinary festivals, with eggs topping the menu. Eggs in every imaginable form, frequently accompanied by pickled herring. In Sweden as in other parts of Europe, boiled eggs with imaginative painted decorations are a vital part of the Easter table.

Good Friday is often a day for salmon – in gravlax, salted, smoked or poached form. Every family has its favourite version. And – who knows? – perhaps the meal will be interrupted by a visit from some of the local children, dressed up as traditional Easter witches, ringing at the door in the hope of cadging candy.

Walpurgis

The Walpurgis celebrations confirm, once and for all, the arrival of spring (though more often than not the weather does its best to contradict), and this of course calls for a party.

All over Sweden on the evening of 30th April, people gather in their thousands to light big bonfires and enjoy the springtime repertoire of (mostly) male voice choirs. Sweden is one of the world's most choral countries, and a ShowTime opportunity like this one is not easily allowed to slip by.

The origins of the bonfire are somewhat of a mystery. Perhaps it was a way of fending off wild animals from the livestock which were put out to pasture at this time, perhaps it was to frighten off witches, or perhaps it was just to keep warm. Either way, the tradition lives on.

Food is also part of the tradition. After the bonfire, the duty of hospitality calls. Why not give them Jansson's Temptation? If prepared in advance, it needs only a few minutes in the oven before the guests take their places. Serve it with crispbread and cheese, a cold beer and a glass – or two – of Swedish vodka.

Walpurgis bonfire

13

Midsummer

This, the most Swedish of annual occasions, comes at the end of June, by which time the sunshine has also reached the northernmost parts of the country and, above the Arctic Circle, the sun never sets. Sweden is now at its loveliest, and Midsummer is everybody's festival.

The celebrations start already the previous evening, when the girls are expected to pick seven different sorts of flowers to put under their pillows, for each one then to dream of the man to be hers. The flowers left over are used to decorate the maypole and make garlands for people and houses alike. The raising of the maypole is the signal for traditional ring dances to the accompaniment of the fiddle, accordion and guitar. The "dance games", as they are called, are often quite ancient and amusing to look at. The one about little frogs, for instance, has to be experienced or witnessed to be believed.

The menu for Midsummer's eve is unwavering: matjes herring, pickled herring, new potatoes cooked in dill, soured cream, chives, crispbread and cheese. Chilled beer and (preferably chillier) Swedish vodka.

Christmas Eve

In Sweden, Father Christmas comes on 24th December, and far too late in the day, if the children are to be believed, because there is a good deal of socialising and gourmandising to be got through before any parcels can be opened. The Swedish Christmas table is a trencherman's eldorado. Its centrepiece is the Christmas ham, which is most often boiled or roasted, with a wonderful grill sauce whose ingredients include mustard and dried bread crumbs. No Christmas table is complete without it. Otherwise the menu can vary. It may include lutfisk – dried saithe or ling, put to soak a week or so before Christmas and then boiled – pigs' trotters and "dip in the pot" (dopp i grytan – the stock from boiling the ham, into which you dip slices of wort bread). But the attractions also include more ordinary things like meatballs, chipolatas, spare ribs, brawn and all manner of pickled herring, as well as bread and cheese, beer and Swedish vodka. The younger members are given a root beer called "julmust" – an ancient tradition which no multinational drinks company in the world can alter. Many people round off the meal with rice porridge. An almond is dropped into the saucepan and whoever finds it on their plate is next in line for the marriage stakes. The plot thickens!

And then at last it is time for Dad to go out for a paper and for Santa in the meantime to put an end to the children's waiting.

Light dishes

"My favourite small dish is potato pancakes – a bird's nest of potato full of good things. But they have to be served with lingonberries. These pancakes are a bit like rösti, except that you make rösti with boiled potatoes.

For a real classic, potato pancakes with pork are the thing. These pancakes are also a good side dish – just the thing to serve with meat, for instance."

Pierre Carlsson
CHEF DE CUISINE, BARKARBY

Crispbread. The Swedish name, "Knäckebröd", says it all. And just try standing on your dignity when eating it! Then there is "Kalles Kaviar", almost like fish in a toothpaste tube. And these two – the crispbread and the Swedish toothpaste caviar – were made for each other. The perfect snack, for one thing.

17

Jansson's Temptation
Serves 4

Ingredients
5-6 POTATOES
2 ONIONS, THINLY SLICED
10 ANCHOVY FILLETS* "ANSJOVIS"
2 TBSPS BUTTER OR MARGARINE
2-3 DL DOUBLE CREAM

Procedure:
Peel the potatoes and cut them into matchstick-sized strips. Put them in cold water. Sauté the onions gently in the butter until they are golden brown. Open the tin of "anchovies", reserving the liquid. Dry the potatoes and put alternate layers of potato, "anchovy" and onion in a greased, oven-proof dish, beginning and ending with a layer of potato. Pour on about half the cream and add a few knobs of butter. Heat in a medium oven (200-225° C) for about 45 minutes. After it has browned nicely, add more cream and, if preferred, a little of the "anchovy" liquid from time to time.

Not really anchovies at all, but spice-cured sprats.
Jansson's Temptation, ready made, is on sale in the shop.

Sun's Eye
Serves 4

Ingredients
4 EGG YOLKS
8 ANCHOVY FILLETS* "ANSJOVIS"
2.4 TBSPS CHOPPED CAPERS
2-4 TBSPS PICKLED BEETROOT, CHOPPED FINE
1 CHOPPED ONION

Procedure:
Chop the "anchovies" fine and place them in a circle. Now add concentric circles of onion, capers and, outermost, beetroot. Serve the egg yolk to one side. Stir at the table.
Alternatively, the mixture can be sautéed in butter and served immediately; it will go very well on a crouton or a slice of toast. The mixture can also be spread on a slice of white bread and then gratinated under the grill or in a hot oven (250° C).

Not really anchovies at all, but spice-cured sprats.

Grandpa's Glory
Serves 4

Ingredients
18-20 ANCHOVY FILLETS* "ANSJOVIS"
1 LARGE ONION
4 HARD-BOILED EGGS
2 TBSPS BUTTER
2 TBSPS CHOPPED PARSLEY
SALT, PEPPER

Procedure:
Dice the "anchovies", onion and eggs. Sauté the onion in the butter until it softens, then add the "anchovies" and eggs. Heat the mixture. Add salt and pepper to taste. Sprinkle with the chopped parsley and serve immediately. Better still with wholemeal bread and a glass of beer.

Not really anchovies at all, but spice-cured sprats.

Jansson's Temptation

Grandpa's Glory

Sun's Eye

Herring au gratin
Serves 4

Ingredients
4 MATJES HERRING FILLETS "MATJESFILÉER"
8 BOILED POTATOES
2 LARGE ONIONS
2 TBSPS CHOPPED DILL
1 TBSP. GRATED CHEESE

Egg custard
3 EGGS
3 DL MILK
SALT, PEPPER

Procedure:
Slice the boiled potatoes. Dice the onion. Put alternate layers of potato, onion and herring in a thoroughly greased oven-proof dish. Pour on the egg custard and sprinkle with the grated cheese. Bake for about 25 minutes at 225° C.

Herring cocktail
Serves 4

Ingredients
1 TIN OF MATJES HERRING FILLETS (200 G) "MATJESFILÉER"
1/2 ICEBERG LETTUCE
1 DL CHOPPED PICKLED BEETROOT "RÖDBETOR"
1 TBSP. CAPERS
1 DL LEEK, CHOPPED FINE

Sauce
1 MINI-TUB OF HORSERADISH SAUCE "PEPPARROTSSÅS"

Garnish
4 EGG YOLKS, RAW

Procedure:
Drain the herring and cut diagonally into centimetre slices. Shred the lettuce, chop the beetroot. Put the lettuce and herring into four individual bowls, then sprinkle with the beetroot, leek and capers. Trail the horseradish sauce. Serve the egg yolks to one side.

Långedrag Salad
Serves 4

Ingredients
1 BIG LETTUCE (ICEBERG, SHREDDED)
1 RED PAPRIKA, THINLY SLICED
1 GREEN PAPRIKA, THINLY SLICED
200 G PEELED SHRIMPS "RÄKOR"
1 LEEK, SHREDDED
2 HARD-BOILED EGGS, HALVED AND QUARTERED
1 JAR BLACK SWEDISH CAVIAR (50 G) "SVART CAVIAR"
1 JAR RED SWEDISH CAVIAR (50 G) "RÖD CAVIAR"
10-20 OLIVES
DILL
1 LEMON, SEGMENTED

Dressing
3 DL CRÈME FRAÎCHE
1 1/2 DL CHILLI SAUCE
1 TBSP. SHERRY
3 TBSPS MAYONNAISE
1 TSP. WORCESTER SAUCE
SALT, PEPPER

Procedure:
Put the shredded lettucee, leek and paprika on a dish or in a salad bowl. Place the shrimps in a long line in the middle. Deposit strips of Swedish caviar to each side of the shrimps, with the egg in between. Garnish with olives, lemon segments and perhaps a sprig or two of dill. Serve the dressing in a separate bowl.

Herring au gratin

Herring cocktail

Långedrag Salad

Småland Herring Salad
Serves 4

Ingredients
1 PIECE OF CUCUMBER
1 SHARP APPLE
1 GREEN PAPRIKA
1 PICKLED GHERKIN
2 TOMATOES
1 TIN OF MATJES HERRING FILLETS (200 G) "MATJESFILÉER"

Dressing
1 ONION, CHOPPED FINE
1 DL PARSLEY, CHOPPED FINE
1 TBSP. VINEGAR
SALT, BLACK PEPPER
1 TSP. WORCESTER SAUCE
3 TBSPS OIL

Procedure:
Peel the cucumber and apple. Cut the cucumber into thin slices and the apple into segments. De-core and chop the apple segments. De-core the paprika and cut into strips. Dice the gherkin and tomatoes. Drain the herring fillets and cut into cm-thick slices. Put all the ingredients in a bowl and stir carefully. Mix the dressing. Add salt and pepper to taste before pouring the dressing over the salad. Store in a cold place for about 30 minutes before serving. Serve with fresh-boiled new potatoes, baked potato or just wholesome bread.

Noggin Salad
Serves 4

Ingredients
1 DL SOURED CREAM "GRÄDDFIL"
1 DL MAYONNAISE
4 TBSPS RED SWEDISH CAVIAR "RÖD CAVIAR"
1 SMALL SPANISH (RED) ONION
1 SMALL (YELLOW) ONION
1 BUNCH OF DILL
1 TIN OF MATJES HERRING FILLETS (200 G) "MATJESFILÉER"
6-7 COLD BOILED POTATOES (500 G APPROX.)
2 HARD-BOILED EGGS, CHOPPED
PARSLEY

Procedure:
Mix the soured cream, mayonnaise and Swedish caviar together. Fold in the onion and dill, chopped fine. Slice the drained matjes fillets and dice the potatoes before adding them to the mixture. Transfer to a bowl. Garnish with chopped egg and parsley. If possible, leave to stand in a cold place for one hour before serving. The perfect "night-cap" with crispbread and a glass of beer.

Småland Herring Salad

Noggin Salad

Matjes Symphony
Serves 4

Ingredients
4-6 MATJES HERRING FILLETS "MATJESFILÉER"
2 HARD-BOILED EGGS
2 PICKLED BEETROOT "RÖDBETOR"
1 BUNCH OF CHIVES
SOURED CREAM "GRÄDDFIL"
ICEBERG LETTUCE

Procedure:
Cut up the drained herrings and put them on a serving dish. Halve the eggs and chop the whites and yolks separately. Fine-chop the beetroot and chives. Garnish the herring in stripes. Serve with soured cream, shredded lettuce, crispbread and cheese.

Anchovy roll
Serves 4

Ingredients for the roll
2 SLICES OF SOFT THIN-BREAD "MJUKT TUNNBRÖD"
1 TIN OF ANCHOVIES* "ANSJOVIS"
1/2 LEEK, SHREDDED
1 ONION, CHOPPED FINE

Not really anchovies at all, but spice-cured sprats.

Ingredients for the scrambled egg
4 EGGS
1 DL MILK OR CREAM
1/2 TSP. SALT

Procedure (scrambled egg):
Beat the eggs, milk/cream and salt together. Melt a little cooking fat in a saucepan or frying pan and pour in the mixture. Heat gently, stirring all the time, till the mixture acquires a creamy consistency.

Final touches:
Butter the bread. Spread the scrambled egg, "anchovies", leek and onion on it, roll up and cut in half. The perfect companion to a good beer.

Anchovy roll

Behold, the full monty of the Swedish herring table, with the Matjes Symphony at the centre of visual and gastronomic attention, flanked by tomato, mustard, plain and onion-flavoured varieties of pickled herring. Cheese, crispbread, beer and Swedish vodka complete the pleasure.

Thin-bread roll with gravlax
Serves 4

Ingredients
2 SLICES OF SOFT THIN-BREAD "MJUKT TUNNBRÖD"
200 G GRAVLAX, SLICED
1 JAR OF GRAVLAX SAUCE "GRAVLAXSÅS"

Procedure:
Butter the bread and add the slices of salmon, covering with the gravlax sauce. Roll up, then cut the rolls into (1-2 cm) slices. Serve as a snack with a drink or a glass of beer.

Thin-bread roll with smoked Swedish reindeer
Serves 4

Ingredients
2 SLICES OF SOFT THIN-BREAD "MJUKT TUNNBRÖD"
1 PACKET OF SMOKED SWEDISH REINDEER "RÖKT RENSTEK"
1 JAR OF HORSERADISH SAUCE "PEPPARROTSSÅS"
A FEW LETTUCE LEAVES

Procedure:
Butter the bread. Place the lettuce leaves on it, followed by the smoked Swedish reindeer, and cover with horse-radish sauce. Roll up, then cut the rolls into (1-2 cm) slices.

Swedish caviar roll
Serves 4

Ingredients
2 SLICES OF SOFT THIN-BREAD "MJUKT TUNNBRÖD"
1 LARGE ONION, CHOPPED FINE
1 JAR OF RED SWEDISH CAVIAR (50 G) "RÖD CAVIAR"
1 DL CRÈME FRAÎCHE
SALT
BLACK PEPPER

Procedure:
Mix the caviar, onion and crème fraîche together. Add a little black pepper and salt to taste. Butter the bread and spread the caviar mixture on it. Roll up and leave in the fridge for at least an hour. Roll up, then cut the rolls into (1-2 cm) slices. Goes nicely with a drink.

These two delicious thin-bread rolls, one with gravlax and the other with smoked Swedish reindeer, go excellently with the caviar roll and the Swedish anchovy roll.

Thin-bread roll with smoked Swedish reindeer
and curry remoulade

Thin-bread basket with shrimp filling

Thin-bread roll with smoked Swedish reindeer and curry remoulade
Serves 4

Ingredients
4 SLICES OF SOFT THIN-BREAD "MJUKT TUNNBRÖD"
100 G CHOPPED PICKLED GHERKIN
2 DL CRÈME FRAÎCHE
1 TSP. CURRY
SALT, BLACK PEPPER
4 POTATOES, BOILED AND SLICED
ICEBERG LETTUCE, SHREDDED
1 PACKET OF SMOKED SWEDISH REINDEER "RÖKT RENSTEK"
1 SPANISH (RED) ONION OR ROASTED ONION, CHOPPED FINE

Procedure:
Mix the gherkin, crème fraîche and curry together. Add salt and pepper to taste. Put the sliced potato on the bread and cover with the curry remoulade. Now add the sliced smoked reindeer, distribute the shredded salad over that and top with the onion. Fold the bread into a cone and add a few blobs of curry remoulade on top. Serve with a glass of beer.

Thin-bread basket with shrimp filling
Serves 4

Ingredients
4 SLICES OF HARD THIN-BREAD "MJUKT TUNNBRÖD"
1 1/2 DL MAYONNAISE
1 1/2 DL CRÈME FRAÎCHE
CHOPPED DILL
1 JAR OF RED SWEDISH CAVIAR (50 G) "RÖD CAVIAR"
LEMON
TOMATO
LETTUCE LEAVES (OPTIONAL)
SALT, PEPPER
1 SPANISH (RED) ONION, CHOPPED FINE
200 G SHRIMPS "RÄKOR"

Procedure:
Put a saucepan with a little water on the hob. Bring to the boil and put a wire rack over the saucepan. Place the hard tunnbröd on the rack and after it has softened, drape it over an inverted glass to form a bowl. When the bread cools its hardness will return and the shrimp mixture can be served in it.

Filling
Mix the mayonnaise with the crème fraîche, the chopped dill and the fine-chopped red onion. Fold in 150 g shrimps, adding salt and pepper to taste. Dole out the mixture into the tunnbröd baskets; a lettuce leaf at the bottom of each basket will keep the bread dry. Distribute the remaining shrimps between the baskets and top with the red bleak roe. Garnish with a slice of lemon, tomato and dill.

Archipelago Herring
Serves 10

Ingredients
2 PKTS OF HÖNÖ (FLAT) BREAD "HÖNÖKAKA"
BUTTER OR MARGARINE
5 DL GRATED "VÄSTERBOTTEN" CHEESE
1 DL ONION, CHOPPED FINE
3 DL SOURED CREAM "GRÄDDFIL"
6 SLICED HARD-BOILED EGGS
WHITE OR BLACK PEPPER
2 DL MAYONNAISE
3 DL ICEBERG LETTUCE, SHREDDED SMALL
1 JAR OF ONION-FLAVOURED PICKLED HERRING (600 G) "LÖKSILL"
1 JAR OF MUSTARD-FLAVOURED PICKLED HERRING (260 G) "SENAPSSILL"
1 JAR OF TOMATO-FLAVOURED PICKLED HERRING (260 G) "TOMATSILL"
1 1/2 DL OF CHIVES, CHOPPED FINE
RINGS OF SPANISH (RED) OR ORDINARY (YELLOW) ONION

Procedure:
Butter two slices of the bread and join them into a round cake. Distribute the grated cheese and the chopped onion on top, then spread with the soured cream. Add two more buttered slices of the bread, taking care not to put the join exactly on top of the previous one. Cover with the sliced egg, add pepper, spread the mayonnaise. Now add the final slices of bread and cover with the fine-shredded lettuce. Cut up the onion herring and make an outer ring of the pieces. Work inwards from there, adding first a ring of mustard herring and lastly a ring of tomato herring in the middle. Garnish with chopped chives and rings of onion.

Salmon and shrimp gâteau
Serves 10

Ingredients
2 PKTS OF HÖNÖ (FLAT) BREAD "HÖNÖKAKA"
400 G SHRIMPS "RÄKOR"
400 G SALMON
400 G MAYONNAISE
4 HARD-BOILED EGGS
CHOPPED DILL
SLICED LEMON
SLICED CUCUMBER
SEGMENTED TOMATO

For the shrimp filling:
Mix 150 g shrimps with 150 g mayonnaise, 1 hard-boiled egg and a little chopped dill.

For the salmon filling:
Chop 150 g salmon into small pieces and mix with 150 g mayonnaise

Procedure:
Join two slices of the bread to form a round cake. Spread the salmon filling and then add two more slices of the bread, taking care not to put the join exactly on top of the previous one. Now spread the shrimp filling and cover with the two remaining slices of bread. Distribute the mayonnaise that is left over, then garnish with shrimps, salmon, boiled egg, lemon, cucumber, tomato and dill.

Archipelago Herring

Salmon and shrimp gâteau

Sandwich gâteau with salmon
Serves 10

Ingredients
2 PKTS OF HÖNÖ (FLAT) BREAD "HÖNÖKAKA"
250 G MAYONNAISE
400 G "GRAVLAX"
4 HARD-BOILED EGGS, HALVED AND QUARTERED
DILL
SLICED LEMON
SEGMENTED TOMATO
SLICED CUCUMBER
1-2 TUBES OF SWEDISH SHRIMP CHEESE "RÄKOST"

For the salmon filling:
Chop 150 g salmon and 1 chopped hard-boiled egg. Mix with 150 g mayonnaise and a little chopped dill.

Procedure:
Join two slices of the bread to form a round cake. Spread with the "shrimp cheese" and cover with two more slices of the bread, with this join at a slight angle to the first one. Spread the salmon filling and cover with the remaining slices of bread. Spread with the mayonnaise and garnish with salmon, egg, lemon, cucumber, tomato and dill.

Hönö Flat-Bread shrimp sandwich
Makes 4

Ingredients
1/2 PKT HÖNÖ (FLAT) BREAD "HÖNÖKAKA"
200 G PEELED SHRIMPS "RÄKOR"
2 HARD-BOILED EGGS
MAYONNAISE
DILL
LEMON
LETTUCE LEAVES

Procedure:
Cut the bread into 4 equal triangles and spread with butter. Garnish with a lettuce leaf (optional). Slice the eggs and distribute on the slices of bread, with blobs of mayonnaise in the middle. Spread the shrimps over the mayonnaise, garnish with lemon slices and dill.

Crispbread with Swedish caviar and egg
Serves 4

Ingredients
4 SLICES OF CRISPBREAD "KNÄCKEBRÖD"
2 HARD-BOILED EGGS, SLICED
1 TUBE OF "KALLES KAVIAR"
CHIVES (OPTIONAL)

Procedure:
Spread the crispbread with butter or margarine, followed by the slices of boiled egg. Squirt the caviar over the eggs. A sprinkle of clipped chives won't do any harm.

Crispbread with Swedish caviar and egg

Crêpes with shrimp filling
Serves 4

Ingredients
1 1/2 DL WHITE FLOUR
1 1/4 DL WATER
1 1/4 DL MILK
2 EGGS
1/2 TSP. SALT
3 TBSPS BUTTER

Alternative: ready-made pancake mixture "Pannkaksmix"

For the filling:
1 TBSP. BUTTER
1 1/2 TBSP. WHITE FLOUR
200 G SHRIMPS "RÄKOR"
1 DL LIQUOR FROM THE SHRIMPS
1 DL WHIPPING CREAM
1 TBSP. DILL, CHOPPED FINE
ABOUT 75 G GRATED CHEESE

Procedure:
Whisk the flour, water and milk into a batter. Work in the eggs, salt and melted better. Leave to stand and swell for 30 minutes, then fry small, delicate crêpes in a frying pan, frying on one side only.

Heat the butter and flour in a saucepan. Stir in liquor and cream with a whisk and cook gently for a few minutes. Add the shrimps and heat without bringing to the boil. Last of all, stir in the dill. Now spread the mixture on the crêpes before rolling them up, fried side outermost. Place them in an oven-proof dish and sprinkle with grated cheese. Brown in the oven at 225° C for 20 or 25 minutes, until the cheese has melted and turned a nice colour.

Caviar crêpes
Serves 4

Ingredients
1 1/2 DL WHITE FLOUR
1 1/4 DL WATER
1 1/4 DL MILK
2 EGGS
1/2 TSP. SALT
3 TBSPS BUTTER

Alternative: ready-made pancake mixture "Pannkaksmix"

For the filling:
2 DL CRÈME FRAÎCHE
2 DL SOURED CREAM "GRÄDDFIL"
1/2 TUBE OF "KALLES KAVIAR"
1/2 LEEK
1 BUNCH OF DILL
WHITE PEPPER
3-4 HARD-BOILED EGGS
1/2 GREEN PAPRIKA
ABOUT 75 G GRATED CHEESE

Whisk the flour, water and milk into a batter. Work in the eggs, salt and melted better. Leave to stand and swell for 30 minutes, then fry small, delicate crêpes in a frying pan, frying on one side only.

Mix the crème fraîche, soured cream and caviar together, adding pepper to taste. Chop the leek, dill, egg and paprika and fold in. Spread the filling on the crêpes and roll them up, fried side outermost. Sprinkle with a little grated cheese and brown in the oven at 225° C for 20 or 25 minutes, until the cheese has melted and turned a nice colour. Serve as a starter or as warm dish together with a good side salad.

Crêpes with shrimp filling   Caviar crêpes

Crab toast
Serves 4

Ingredients
4 SLICES OF BREAD, BROWN OR WHITE
1 TUBE OF CRAB PASTE "KRABBPASTEJ"
5 TBSPS COTTAGE CHEESE
5 TBSPS CRÈME FRAÎCHE
3 TBSPS DILL, CHOPPED FINE
SALT, PEPPER
LETTUCE LEAVES
4 SLICES OF LEMON
1 JAR OF BLACK SWEDISH CAVIAR (50 G) "SVART CAVIAR"

Procedure:
Mix the cottage cheese and crème fraîche in a food processor or press through a sieve. Add the crab paste. Using a food processor, you get a nice, fluffy mixture. Add dill, salt and pepper to taste. Put a lettuce leaf on each slice of bread, followed by the crab mixture. Finish off with a large dob of black Swedish caviar and garnish with a slice of lemon.

Cold summer soup with shrimps
Serves 4

Ingredients
5 DL YOGHURT AU NATUREL
3 DL WATER
1 CUCUMBER, DICED
1 CLOVE OF GARLIC, CRUSHED
1 DL CHIVES, CHOPPED FINE
1/2 TSP. SALT
1 SALT SPOON OF BLACK PEPPER
200 G PEELED SHRIMPS "RÄKOR"

Procedure:
Mix the yoghurt, water, cucumber, garlic and chives together in a bowl. Stir well to mix properly. Add salt and pepper to taste. Distribute the shrimps in individual bowls and pour on the soup. An ice cube in each bowl is a good idea. Serve with white bread.

Crab toast

Cold summer soup with shrimps

Baked potato with dill-flavoured pickled herring
Serves 4

Ingredients
4 LARGE BAKED POTATOES
1 JAR OF DILL-FLAVOURED PICKLED HERRING (275 G) "DILLSILL"
3 DL CRÈME FRAÎCHE
2 SALT SPOONS OF BLACK PEPPER
2 TBSPS CHOPPED DILL AND PARSLEY

Procedure:
Pour the crème fraîche into a bowl and flavour with salt, pepper parsley and dill. Brush, rinse and dry the potatoes. Prick or slash the peel before putting the potatoes in an oven-proof dish or microwave dish. Bake in the oven at 225° C for about 50 or 60 minutes (or micro for 15-25 minutes at full power). Accompany with the dill-herring, cut in pieces, and the soured cream. With lettuce and bread thrown in – lunch!

Baked potato with shrimp filling
Serves 4

Ingredients
4 LARGE BAKED POTATOES
1 JAR OF RED SWEDISH CAVIAR (50 G) "RÖD CAVIAR"
200 G PEELED SHRIMPS "RÄKOR"
2 DL CRÈME FRAÎCHE
3-5 DL CHOPPED DILL
1 SPANISH (RED) ONION
SALT AND PEPPER

Procedure:
Wash the potatoes and bake them until soft in the oven at 225° C for about 50 or 60 minutes or in the microwave on full power. Chop the red onion very small and mix with the roe and shrimps. Now fold in the crème fraîche and the chopped dill. Add salt and pepper to taste, then leave to stand in the fridge for an hour or so. When the potatoes are done, cut a cross on top of each one, then squeeze the sides to open the potato and make room for the shrimp mixture. A sprig of dill makes a nice garnish.

Party Spuds with black Swedish caviar
Serves 4

Ingredients
4 LARGE POTATOES
OIL
SALT
1 JAR OF BLACK SWEDISH CAVIAR (50 G) "SVART CAVIAR"
1 LEMON, SLICED
DILL
1 1/2 DL CRÈME FRAÎCHE

Procedure:
Wash the potatoes thoroughly and cut them into 2 cm thick slices. Put the slices on a wire rack or straight into a greased oven-proof dish. Oil and salt them lightly. Brown in the oven at 200° C for about 20 or 25 minutes. Transfer to a serving dish and add a blob of caviar to each slice. Top with a little crème fraîche and garnish with a slice of lemon and dill. This makes a good suppertime treat, and it goes well with fish.

Potato pancakes with red and black Swedish caviar
Serves 4

Ingredients
4-6 PEELED POTATOES
1/2 TSP. SALT
1 SALT SPOON OF WHITE PEPPER
25 G BUTTER
1 JAR OF BLACK SWEDISH CAVIAR (50 G) "SVART CAVIAR"
1 JAR OF RED SWEDISH CAVIAR (50 G) "RÖD CAVIAR"
1 SPANISH (RED) ONION, CHOPPED FINE
2 DL CRÈME FRAÎCHE
LETTUCE LEAVES AND DILL FOR GARNISH

Procedure:
Grate the peeled potatoes with a grating iron, then mix with salt and pepper. Now fry them in butter to make crisp cakes of pancake thinness. Serve immediately, on the plates, with a blob of crème fraîche on each cake and dobs of red and black caviar to each side.
Garnish with the lettuce, sprinkle with fine-chopped red onion and finish off with a sprig of dill.

Salmon recipes

"Gravlax is typical Swedish fare. People who've never had it before think it's raw fish, but it isn't: it's marinated in a mixture of salt, sugar, dill, white pepper and allspice – very convenient and useful raw material. Traditionally, gravlax is served with a mustard sauce, but the variations are unlimited."

Lennarth Brewitz
CHEF DE CUISINE AND PRODUCT DEVELOPER

Gravlax today is a Swedish delicacy with a worldwide following.

Mustard-grilled gravlax with "anchovy" butter
Serves 4

Ingredients
400 G "GRAVLAX"
1 EGG YOLK
2 TBSPS SWEDISH MUSTARD "SENAP"
1/2 DL DRIED BREAD CRUMBS
1 SALT SPOON OF POTATO FLOUR
100 G BUTTER
2 SPANISH (RED) ONIONS, CHOPPED FINE
2 1/2 DL RED WINE
50 G ANCHOVY* FILLETS "ANSJOVIS"
WHITE PEPPER

Swedish anchovies - spice-cured sprats

For the grill sauce:
Mix the mustard with the egg yolk and potato flour.

For the "anchovy" butter:
Boil the chopped onion in the red wine and "anchovy" liquor until nearly all the liquid has been absorbed. Leave to cool before creaming together with the butter and the chopped "anchovies". Add pepper to taste.

Procedure:
Place the gravlax slices overlapping in a greased, oven-proof dish. Spread the grill sauce over them and sprinkle with the bread crumbs. Grill in the oven until golden brown; this takes 5 or 10 minutes at 200° C. Serve with the "anchovy" butter to one side.

Cold poached salmon with bleak roe sauce
Serves 4

Ingredients
2 PKTS SALMON FILLET PIECES (4 X 125 G) "LAXFILÉ"
2 1/2 DL CRÈME FRAÎCHE
1 JAR OF RED SWEDISH CAVIAR (50 G) "RÖD CAVIAR"
CHOPPED DILL
DIJON MUSTARD
POTATO
SALT, PEPPER
SLICED LEMON

Court bouillon (poaching liquid)
1 1/2 DL WATER
1 DL WHITE WINE VINEGAR
2 TBSPS SALT
5 CORNS OF ALLSPICE
2 CORNS OF WHITE PEPPER
1 BAY LEAF
1 CARROT
1 ONION
DILL

Procedure:
Start by making the court bouillon. Cut up the carrot and onion and put them in a saucepan with the dill and spices. Pour on the water and vinegar and boil for about 15 minutes. Put the salmon pieces into a saucepan and strain the poaching liquid over them. Bring the salmon to the boil and cook for 3-5 minutes. Now leave it to cool in the liquid before putting it in the fridge for the night. Mix the crème fraîche, roe, dill and Dijon mustard together. Add salt and pepper to taste. To bring out the full flavour of the sauce, make it one day in advance. Serve the salmon, garnished with lemon and dill, with the roe sauce and fresh-boiled potatoes.

Mustard-grilled gravlax with "anchovy" butter

Cold poached salmon with bleak roe sauce

Poached fillet of salmon with browned slices of apple and artichoke sauce

Serves 4

Ingredients

2 PKTS SALMON FILLETS (4 X 125 G) "LAXFILÉ"
3 DL WATER
1 LEMON
1 APPLE
1 TSP. SALT
10 CORNS OF WHITE PEPPER

For the artichoke sauce:

2 HG ARTICHOKES (2 MEDIUM-SIZED ONES)
2 DL WHIPPING CREAM
STOCK FROM THE FISH

Procedure:

De-core and slice the apple and brown the slices carefully. Pour the water into a sauté pan and put in a few slices of lemon, the peppercorns and the salt. Turn up the heat so that the water boils gently. Put in the fillets of salmon and poach them (cook gently) for 8-12 minutes. Remove the salmon and strain the stock. Boil the artichokes in the stock for 20 or 30 minutes, until they feel soft. Strain them and run them to a purée in the food processor. Boil the cream and purée, adding enough stock to give the right consistency. Add salt and pepper, and serve with freshly boiled potatoes.

Salmon coated with dill and lemon
Serves 4

Ingredients
2 PKTS PIECES OF SALMON FILLETS (4 X 125 G) "LAXFILÉ"
50 G DILL
100 G DRIED BREADCRUMBS
1 LEMON
1 TIN OF SWEDISH ANCHOVY FILLETS (100 G) "ANSJOVIS"
20 G BROWN MUSTARD SEEDS
1/3 L FISH STOCK
150 G BUTTER
CORN FLOUR
1 KG POTATOES
8 FRESH BEETROOT
SALT, PEPPER

Procedure:
Chop the dill, grate the lemon peel and mix with the bread crumbs. Coat the top side of the salmon with the dill and lemon mixture. Boil the beetroot till soft in lightly salted water, then put to one side. Bring the stock to the boil before putting in the chopped Swedish anchovies and the mustard seeds. Keep on the boil until the mustard seeds have softened, then thicken the sauce with the corn flour and, stirring all the time, add 100 g of the butter. Add salt and pepper to taste. Peel the boiled beetroot and cut them into segments. Salt and pepper them before frying them in butter. Fry the salmon slowly in butter, starting with the coated sides. Salt and pepper, then turn the fish over and finish frying. Put the beetroot on a place with the fish on top. Pour the sauce all round and serve with boiled potatoes.

Irene's Salmon Casserole
Serves 4

Ingredients
400 G POTATOES
2 PKTS PIECES OF SALMON FILLETS (4 X 125 G) "LAXFILÉ"
1 BUNCH OF DILL
2 TBSPS OIL
3/4 DL WHITE WINE
1/2 DL SHERRY
1-2 TSPS SALT
SOURED CREAM "GRÄDDFIL"
GRATED HORSERADISH

Procedure:
Peel and slice the potatoes. Salt the pieces of salmon lightly, divide them down the middle and put alternate layers of salmon and dill + potato into an oven-proof dish or casserole. Heat the oil slightly and pour it over the salmon and potato. Salt and cover. Leave in the oven for about 20 or 30 minutes at 175° C. Pour on the wine and sherry when the potato is soft and leave in the oven for about two minutes. Serve with soured cream, flavoured with grated horseradish.

Irene's Salmon Casserole

Salmon coated with dill and lemon

Ginger-glazed fillet of salmon with warm potato salad
Serves 4

Ingredients
2 PKTS OF SALMON FILLETS (4 X 125 G) "LAXFILÉ"
400 G POTATOES, BOILED AND SLICED
1 LEEK, CUT DIAGONALLY INTO THIN SLICES
1 MEDIUM-LARGE CHINESE CABBAGE, SHREDDED
SALT, BLACK PEPPER
DILL

For the glaze:
1/2 DL SUGAR
1 DL APPLE CIDER VINEGAR
4 DL CHICKEN STOCK OR SUCHLIKE
50 G FRESH GINGER, PEELED AND SHREDDED FINE
1 CLOVE OF GARLIC, PRESSED
1 TBSP. SPANISH PEPPER
CORN FLOUR
SALT

Procedure:
Melt the sugar to a pale caramel in a saucepan. Add the vinegar and stock. Boil briskly, skim and add the ginger, the garlic and the Spanish pepper. Boil for about 15 or 20 minutes. Add salt to taste and thicken to the right consistency with corn flour. Salt the pieces of salmon and put them into an ovenproof dish. Brown in the oven at 200° C for about 8-12 minutes. Brown the potato, leek and Chinese cabbage lightly in a little butter over a low flame. Add salt and pepper to taste. Make a bed of the warm potato salad on the plate, with the salmon on top, and pour the ginger glaze over it. Garnish with a sprig of dill. A green vegetable makes a good companion piece.

Ginger-glazed fillet of salmon with warm potato salad

Meatball recipes

"Meatballs have to be just the right size – not too big and not too small – and served with a real cream sauce. Not much pepper in the sauce, but plenty in the meatballs themselves. I never tire of them.

One good thing about meatballs is their many uses. Warm, cold, in baguettes, in ordinary sandwiches, perhaps with salted gherkins. Perfect with apple chutney, with a little chilli and moussaka. Or with an ordinary potatoes au gratin.

But the real classic, of course, is meatballs with boiled potatoes, cream sauce and lingonberry jam. An unbeatable combination!"

Peter Carlström
CHEF DE CUISINE AND PRODUCT RANGE MANAGER HELSINGBORG

Meatballs are pure, no-nonsense food, and IKEA's are made in the traditional way – with no preservatives added, for example. When making your own, don't forget the allspice. Otherwise the shop ones are always a handy and tasty solution.

Meatballs with cream sauce
Serves 4

30-40 SWEDISH MEATBALLS "KÖTTBULLAR"

Procedure:
Heat the meatballs as per the instructions on the package.
(Ready-made sauce "Gräddsås" is also obtainable.)

If you prefer making your own meatballs:
250 G MINCED BEEF
250 G MINCED PORK
1 EGG
2-3 DL CREAM AND WATER (OR MILK AND WATER)
2 1/2 TBSP. ONION, CHOPPED FINE
1/2 DL UNSWEETENED RUSK FLOUR
2 COLD BOILED POTATOES
4-5 TBSPS BUTTER, MARGARINE OR OIL
SALT, WHITE PEPPER (ALLSPICE)

Procedure:
Heat the onion till golden in a couple of tbsps of lightly
browned butter, mash the potatoes and moisten the rusk
flour in a little water. Mix all the ingredients into a
smooth farce of the right consistency and flavour gener-
ously with salt, white pepper and (optional) a little fine-
crushed allspice.
Using a pair of spoons rinsed in water, shape the farce
into relatively large, round balls and transfer to a floured
chopping board, then fry them quite slowly in plenty of
butter.

For the sauce:
1 DL CREAM
2 DL WATER OR BEEF STOCK
CHINESE SOY
(1 TBSP. WHITE FLOUR)
SALT, WHITE PEPPER

Procedure:
Swirl out the pan with a couple of dl boiling water or
meat stock. Strain the pan juices and dilute with cream.
Thicken with white flour if preferred. Season well, and
serve this and the meatballs with freshly boiled potatoes,
uncooked lingonberry jam, a green salad and salted or
pickled gherkins.

Meatballs with cabbage cooked in cream and Spanish (red) onion
Serves 4

Ingredients
30-40 MEATBALLS "KÖTTBULLAR"
600 G CABBAGE (WHITE CABBAGE, RED CABBAGE OR SAVOY)
1 SPANISH (RED) ONION
1 CLOVE OF GARLIC
4 DL CREAM
1-2 TSPS SALT
WHITE PEPPER, GROUND
1-2 TSP. SUGAR
1 TBSP. LEMON JUICE
LINGONBERRY JAM "LINGONSYLT"

Procedure:
Roughly dice all the cabbage and shred the red onion.
Add the pressed clove of garlic. Boil everything in the
cream until soft. Add salt, pepper, sugar and lemon to
taste. Meantime, heat the meatballs as per the instructions on the package.
Put a small quantity of the stewed cabbage onto the plates, with the meatballs on top. Serve with riced potato or
pasta and – the master touch – a spoonful of lingonberry
jam.

Meatballs with cabbage cooked in
cream and Spanish (red) onion

Meatballs with cream sauce

Meatball kebab
Serves 4

Ingredients
24 MEATBALLS "KÖTTBULLAR"
6-8 COLD POTATOES
1 ONION
4 SKEWERS OR PLANT PINS
2 PAPRIKAS

For the salad:
4 DIFFERENT KINDS OF LETTUCE
1 CUCUMBER
4 TOMATOES

For the dressing:
3 TBSPS SWEDISH MUSTARD "SENAP"
1 DL SINGLE CREAM

Procedure:
Divide each potato down the middle after cutting off the ends. Divide each paprika
in six and each onion in four. Now thread meatballs, potato, onion and paprika
alternately onto the skewers. Brush the skewers with a little oil and brown them
under the grill or in the frying pan. Rinse the salad and put out on four plates.
Shred the cucumber and sprinkle over the salad. Whisk the mustard and cream
together and pour over. When the kebabs are ready, put them on top and serve
immediately.

Meatball casserole with apples
Serves 4

Ingredients

30-40 READY-MADE MEATBALLS "KÖTTBULLAR"
3 APPLES
4 POTATOES
400 G WHITE CABBAGE
1 TSP. SUGAR
1 CUBE OF CHICKEN OR BEEF STOCK
3 DL CIDER
MILLED ALLSPICE
SALT

Procedure:

Peel the potatoes, roughly slicing both them and the cabbage. Peel and de-core the apples and cut them into segments. Heat the potatoes and cabbage in a little butter. Add the sugar and continue heating until the mixture colours a little. Add the segments of apple and heat for another minute or so. Add the cider and stock cube. Add salt and allspice to taste and cook for about 5 minutes. Fry the meatballs as per the instructions on the package. Add them when ready and cook for another 5 minutes. Serve the casserole in deep plates; crispbread makes a good accessory.

Sausage recipes

"Falun sausage always evokes the memory of my grandmother's fried Falun sausage and stewed macaroni. Every time I catch the scent I'm transported back in time and space to her kitchen.

Falun sausage is an easy raw material to work with. It turns out well however you treat it. You can use it for starters, main courses – almost for desserts. Just cut up or turned into something approaching a gourmet dinner à la tournedos. It never lets you down."

Jens Thunström
CHEF DE CUISINE, GOTHENBURG

The variations are infinite, added to which, Falun sausage – cooked or raw – has a long fridge life. And it's a real cross-over product, equally compatible with the European and Asian cuisines. Wok-fry it or use it for Stroganoff or kebabs.

Boiled Falun sausage with riced potatoes
Serves 4

Ingredients
1 FALUN SAUSAGE (400 G) "FALUKORV"
1 BOTTLE OF BEER
1 SALT SPOONFUL OF COARSE-MILLED WHITE PEPPER
SALT
100 G SHREDDED LEEK
50 G COARSE-GRATED HORSERADISH

Procedure:
Remove the skin from the sausage. Cut the sausage into thick slices, transfer these to a greased oven-proof dish and pour on enough beer to cover the sausage about half-way. Sprinkle with coarse-milled white pepper and a little salt. Cover over with foil and cook in the oven at 250° C for about 15 or 20 minutes. Now sprinkle with the freshly grated horseradish and the leek. Serve with freshly cooked, riced potatoes.

Roast Falun sausage with diced potato and
tomato

Falun sausage stuffed with cheese

Roast Falun sausage with diced potato and tomato
Serves 4

Ingredients
1 FALUN SAUSAGE (400 G) "FALUKORV"
600 G POTATO
2 TBSPS BUTTER OR OIL
1 TSP. SALT
1 SALT SPOONFUL OF BLACK PEPPER
1/2 TSP. PAPRIKA POWDER
1 ONION
4 TBSPS CHILLI SAUCE/TOMATO KETCHUP
2 TBSPS TOMATO PURÉE
1 TSP. THYME

Procedure:
Peel and dice the potatoes, then parboil for 3-4 minutes before transferring to a greased dish. Add salt and pepper and sprinkle with the paprika powder. Add the rest of the butter in dobs and roast in the oven for about 10 minutes at 250° C. Meantime, slice the (skinned) Falun sausage. Chop the onion and mix it with the chilli sauce and tomato purée. Place the sausage on top of the potato and spread the onion and tomato mixture over it. Sprinkle with thyme before putting the dish back in the oven for another 10 minutes.

Falun sausage stuffed with cheese
Serves 4

Ingredients
1 FALUN SAUSAGE (400 G) "FALUKORV"
150 G "HERRGÅRD" CHEESE
4 LARGE TOMATOES
8 SMALL ONIONS
2 TBSPS BUTTER
2 TBSPS SWEDISH MUSTARD "SENAP"
1-2 TBSPS WATER OR BEEF STOCK
SALT, WHITE PEPPER (GARLIC POWDER)

Procedure:
Skin the sausage and cut it into cm-thick slices, but not quite all the way through. Cut the cheese into thin slices and spread with mustard on both sides. Insert the cheese between the sausage slices. Peel and parboil the onions. Carefully place the "larded" sausage in a well-greased, oven-proof dish together with the onions and the tomatoes, whole or halved. Sprinkle with the spices and add a few knobs of butter (a little garlic on the tomatoes makes a fine contrast). Roast in the oven for about 25-30 minutes at 250° C or until the cheese has melted and the whole thing is a nice colour and thoroughly cooked. If it looks dry, pour on a little more stock or water. Serve with potatoes – either riced or fried raw.

Cabbage soup with Falun sausage
Serves 4

Ingredients
1 FALUN SAUSAGE (400 G) "FALUKORV"
800 G DICED WHITE CABBAGE
3 SLICED CARROTS
5 SLICES POTATOES
1 LEEK
1 3/4 LITRES OF WATER
10 WHOLE ALLSPICE CORNS
SALT
CHOPPED PARSLEY

Procedure:
Skin the Falun sausage and cut it into cm-thick slices. Put them into a stew pot together with the spices and water and bring to the boil. Remove the sausage after cooking for 1-2 minutes. Put in the diced cabbage, potato and carrots. Bring to the boil and cook for 2-4 minutes before adding the leek, cut in slices. Cook the soup on a low flame for 10-15 minutes until the vegetables are soft, then replace the sausage and boil briskly for a minute or so. Sprinkle with the chopped parsley and serve with a little Swedish mustard; a piece of Hönö bread or crispbread goes very well with this soup.

Wok-fried Falun sausage with yoghurt sauce
Serves 4

Ingredients
1 FALUN SAUSAGE (400 G) "FALUKORV"
3 CARROTS
1 SPANISH (RED) ONION
100 G MANGE-TOUT
100 G MINI-MAIZE
50 G BEAN SHOOTS
CHINESE SOY
1 SALT SPOONFUL OF GROUND GINGER
COOKING OIL
1 BEEF STOCK CUBE
3 DL WATER
2 TBSPS TOMATO PURÉE
2-3 TBSPS POTATO FLOUR
1-2 TBSPS HONEY
SAMBAL OELEK
SALT, PEPPER

Yoghurt sauce
200 G COARSE-GRATED CUCUMBER
SALT
2 DL YOGHURT
1 TBSP. CHOPPED PARSLEY
1/2 TSP. BLACK PEPPER

Procedure:
Shred the (skinned) sausage and carrots and slice the leek. Heat them in cooking oil together with a little soy and ginger. Mix the beef stock, tomato purée, potato flour and honey together. Add the mixture of sausage and carrots together with the other green vegetables. Heat everything thoroughly. Add Sambal oelek, salt and pepper to taste.

Serve the wok with the yoghurt sauce and freshly cooked rice.

For the yoghurt sauce
Sprinkle the grated cucumber with a little salt and leave to stand for about 20 minutes before squeezing out as much juice as possible. Mix the cucumber with the yoghurt and parsley and add black pepper to taste.

Cabbage soup with Falun sausage

Wok-fried Falun sausage with yoghurt sauce

Isterband sausage with stewed potato

Grilled Isterband sausage with potato salad

Isterband sausage with stewed potato
Serves 4

Ingredients
1 PKT SWEDISH BARLEY SAUSAGE (4 PIECES) "ISTERBAND"
10 BOILED POTATOES
2 TBSPS BUTTER
2 TBSPS WHITE FLOUR
1 TSP. SALT
4 DL MILK
WHITE PEPPER

Procedure:
Put the Isterband sausage in an oven-proof dish and roast for 10 or 15 minutes at 225° C. Meanwhile start by slicing the boiled potatoes. Melt the butter and stir in the white flour with a whisk. Dilute with the milk until you have a sauce of the right thickness. Cook for 3-5 minutes. Add salt and pepper to taste. Stir in the potato and warm the mixture thoroughly. Serve the stewed potato with the Isterband sausage. Pickled beetroot are a good accompaniment.

Grilled Isterband sausage with potato salad
Serves 4

Ingredients
1 PKT SWEDISH BARLEY SAUSAGE (4 PIECES) "ISTERBAND"
600 G SLICED COLD BOILED POTATO
1/2 LEEK, SHREDDED
1-2 SLICED SPANISH (RED) ONIONS
100 G SHREDDED SMOKED SWEDISH REINDEER "RÖKT RENSTEK"
(ALTERNATIVELY, 100 G SHREDDED BACON)
1 TBSP. CAPERS
1 TBSP. DILL, CHOPPED FINE
1 TBSP. PARSLEY, CHOPPED FINE
SLICED PICKLED BEETROOT "RÖDBETOR"

For the vinaigrette
1/2 DL SWEDISH MUSTARD "SENAP"
2 TBSPS VINEGAR
1/2 DL COOKING OIL
1/2 TBSP. SUGAR
SALT
MILLED WHITE PEPPER

Procedure:
Steam the sliced potato by boiling a little water in a saucepan, putting the potatoes into a colander and then lowering this into the saucepan. Cover and steam for 3-5 minutes, then mix the potato with the leek, the red onion, the smoked reindeer and the capers, dill and parsley. Meanwhile grill the Isterband sausages (or roast them in the oven). When they are done, part them down the middle. Put out the lukewarm potato salad onto plates and pour the vinaigrette over it. Place the split sausages on top of the potato salad, serve with pickled beetroot.

Bacon roulade stuffed with Viennese sausage
Serves 4

Ingredients
6-8 VIENNESE SAUSAGES OR ORDINARY HOT DOGS "VARMKORV"
6-8 THIN SLICES OF BACON
150 "HERRGÅRD" OR SIMILAR CHEESE
1-2 DL LAGER
1-2 TBSPS SWEDISH MUSTARD "SENAP"

Procedure:
Make an incision along each sausage and spread the opening with mustard. Cut the cheese into narrow strips the same length as the incision in the sausages, putting one strip in each sausage. Wrap the sausages in thin slices of bacon, transfer them to an oven-proof dish and roast them in the oven for 15 or 20 minutes at 250° C, until the bacon is crisp and the sausages are thoroughly hot. Dilute with lager during the last few minutes. Serve the roulades on their own, e.g. as an after-theatre snack, or with boiled rice or riced potatoes.

Hot sausage hash
Serves 4

Ingredients
6-8 RAW POTATOES
1 ONION
1 CLOVE OF GARLIC
2 RED PAPRIKAS
COOKING OIL
1 FALUN SAUSAGE (400 G) "FALUKORV"
1 TIN OF KIDNEY BEANS (400 G APPROX.)
1 TSP. SALT
CHILLI SAUCE
CRÈME FRAÎCHE

Procedure:
Dice the (peeled) potatoes, onion and paprika and heat together in a frying pan for about 5 minutes. Dice the (skinned) Falun sausage the same as the potatoes. Rinse the kidney beans under the tap. Stir them and the sausage into the potato and paprika in the frying pan. Flavour with one pressed clove of garlic and salt, and leave to dry for about 5-10 minutes. Serve with a strong chilli sauce and – why not?! – a blob of crème fraîche.

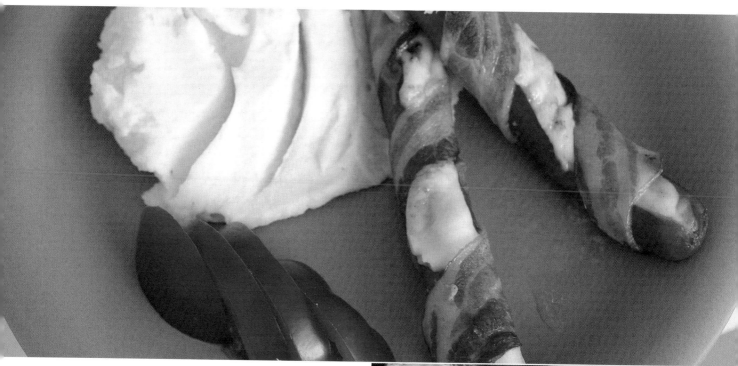

Bacon roulade stuffed with Viennese sausage

Hot sausage hash

Desserts

"The first time I came across lingonberries I was enchanted by their beautiful colour and their wonderful acidulous quality. I mainly use them for traditional Swedish recipes like meatballs and potato pancakes, but they also make excellent desserts. I just can't think of a better combination of Swedish and French cuisine than a lingonberry parfait."

Maxime Cancade
RESTAURANT MANAGER, STRASBOURG

Lingonberries have been called "the red gold of Sweden". They are widespread in forests all over the country, but commonest in the north. IKEA's uncooked lingonberries, being more mildly flavoured than others, are also ideal for desserts.

Lingonberry parfait
Serves 4-6

Ingredients
2 EGGS
1/2 DL SUGAR
1 1/2 DL LINGONBERRY JAM "LINGONSYLT"
3 DL WHIPPING CREAM
WHIPPING CREAM AND LINGONBERRY JAM FOR GARNISH

Procedure:
Beat the eggs and sugar till fluffy. Carefully fold in the lingonberry jam. Whisk the cream quite hard and fold not quite all of it into the egg mixture. Freeze the mixture in individual glasses or a dish. Leave to stand in the freezer for at least 4 hours. Remove the parfait from the freezer 5 or 10 minutes before serving. Garnish with a blob of cream topped with lingonberry jam.

Crunchy lingonberry ice cream
Serves 8

Ingredients
2 WHITES OF EGG
2 EGG YOLKS
1/2 DL ICING SUGAR
1 JAR OF LINGONBERRY JAM (400 G) "LINGONSYLT"
1/2 DL GIN OR ESSENCE
ABOUT 30 SMALL MERINGUES
3 DL WHIPPING CREAM

To serve:
Lightly sugared lingonberries

Procedure:
Beat the whites and cream separately until stiff. Beat the yolks and icing sugar to a fluffy mixture. Fold in the lingonberries, gin and cream. Lastly, and carefully, add the egg whites. Pour half the mixture into a ring tin, poke the meringues into it and then add the remainder of the mixture. Cover the tin with foil and leave in the freezer for at least 4 hours. Remove from the freezer 30 minutes before serving. Turn out the ice cream onto a serving dish and garnish with lingonberries. This ice cream can be served with sauce if preferred, in which case, hollow out a few passion fruit and mix the flesh with undiluted, concentrated lingonberry squash.

Lingonberry cream with rusks
Serves 4

Ingredients
10 SWEDISH RUSKS "SKORPOR"
3 DL WHIPPING CREAM
1 – 1 1/2 DL LINGONBERRY JAM "LINGONSYLT"

Procedure:
Whip the cream to a moderate thickness. Stir in half the lingonberry jam. Put alternate layers of rusks and "lingonberry cream" into a bowl. Garnish with the remainder of the jam. Leave the cream to stand in the fridge for 10 or 15 minutes, to soften the rusks a little. This is a plain, refreshing dessert. Something else that goes down very well is ice cream cones filled with "lingonberry cream", topped with a dash of lingonberry jam.

Cheese ice cream
Serves 4

Ingredients
3 DL WHIPPING CREAM
1 TSP. VANILLA SUGAR
3 EGG WHITES
3 EGG YOLKS
1 1/2 DL SUGAR
100 G PHILADELPHIA CREAM CHEESE
6 "DIGESTIVE" BISCUITS
FRESH BERRIES FOR GARNISH

Procedure:
Beat the cream and vanilla sugar till stiff. Whisk the egg yolks, sugar and Philadelphia Cream Cheese in another bowl until fluffy. Beat the egg whites separately until they stiffen. Now mix everything together. Crumble three Digestive biscuits into a tin, pour on the mixture and crumble the remaining biscuits over it. Leave in the freezer for at least 4 hours. Remove from the freezer 20 or 30 minutes before serving and garnish with fresh berries.

Fluffy cheesecake
Serves 4

Ingredients
2 TBSPS BUTTER OR MARGARINE
2 TBSPS WHITE FLOUR
3 DL WHIPPING CREAM
4 EGGS
3 DL GRATED "HERRGÅRD" CHEESE
BLUEBERRY AND RASPBERRY JAM "DROTTNINGSYLT"

Procedure:
Warm the oven to 200° C. Heat the cooking fat in a saucepan. Add the flour and stir. Add the cream, stirring all the time, and cook for about 3 minutes. Stir the egg yolks and cheese into the mixture and allow to cool slightly. Beat the egg whites to a hard froth and fold them carefully into the mixture. Transfer to a greased, oven-proof dish and bake for about 30 minutes. Serve lukewarm as a dessert, together with berries or jam.

Fluffy cheesecake

Cheese ice cream

Scanian apple pie and custard

Cinnamon pancake with honeyed apple

Scanian apple pie and custard
Serves 4

Ingredients
6 APPLES
2 DL DRIED BREAD CRUMBS
1 DL SUGAR
3 TBSPS BUTTER OR MARGARINE
1/2 DL WATER
CINNAMON (OPTIONAL)

For the custard:
2 EGG WHITES
2 EGG YOLKS
2 TBSPS SUGAR
2 DL WHIPPING CREAM
1 1/2 TBSPS VANILLA SUGAR
OR: CUSTARD POWDER ETC. "MARSÁNSÅS", AS PER
INSTRUCTIONS ON THE PACKET.

Procedure:
Heat the oven to 200° C. Peel the apples, de-core them
and slice thinly. Make alternate layers of dried bread
crumbs, apple, sugar and (optional) a little cinnamon) in
a greased, oven-proof dish, topping off with more bread
crumbs. Scatter blobs of butter/margarine over this before pouring on the water. Bake on the middle shelf of
the oven for about 30 minutes. Serve with custard.

To make the custard:
Separate the yolks and whites of the eggs. Beat the yolks
and sugar till fluffy. Whisk the cream and vanilla sugar
together and add to the egg mixture, then add the (stiffly
beaten) egg whites.

Cinnamon pancake with honeyed apple
Serves 4

Ingredients
1 PKT PANCAKE MIX "PANNKAKSMIX"
2 TSPS GROUND CINNAMON
VANILLA ICE CREAM OR WHIPPING CREAM
ICING SUGAR

For the honeyed apple:
3 MEDIUM-SIZED APPLES
2 TBSPS BUTTER
2 TBSPS HONEY
1 TBSP. LEMON JUICE

Procedure:
Whisk the pancake mix as instructed on the packet. Beat
in the cinnamon and leave the batter to stand in the fridge for half an hour or so. De-core the apples and cut
them into segments, which you then heat in a little butter. Stir in the honey and lemon juice and leave on a low
flame (not too hot – you don't want the apple segments
to disintegrate). Now bake the pancakes in the oven and
serve them folded on a plate, together with the honeyed
apple and, even better, a little ice cream or whipped
cream. Prettify the pancakes by dusting with a little icing
sugar.

Drinks

Sweden is part of the so-called Vodka Belt, a position to which it has done more than justice over the centuries. In our own time, though, spirits and civilisation have come closer together, and Swedish vodka, for instance, now ranks as a gourmet science in its own right. A lot of Swedes have their own special mixtures, flavouring their brännvin with everything from Seville orange zest and vine leaves to St John's wort and wormwood. Swedish vodka has to be served chilled, and with meals.

Beer too has a long Swedish history, dating back to the mead of the Viking era. Today's selection, Heaven be praised, is more conducive to conviviality than bloodletting on gastronomic occasions.

The non-alcoholic department of the Swedish larder has by tradition had a wide range of squashes and juices – one way of conserving the harvest of fruit and berries for the long winter ahead. Elderflower and lingonberry squash are two Swedish specialities.

And don't forget the Christmas root beer, "julmust" – a favourite with all Swedish children and by far the most popular of Yuletide soft drinks.

Christmas Vodka
70 cl

1 BOTTLE (70 CL) OF VODKA
2 TBSPS GRANULATED SUGAR
2 STICKS OF CINNAMON
12 WHOLE CLOVES
12 WHOLE CARDAMOM SEEDS
1 ORANGE

Procedure:
Put 2 tbsps granulated sugar, 2 sticks of cinnamon, 12 whole cloves and 12 whole cardamom seeds into a litre bottle. Pour on the contents of a 70 cl bottle of vodka, cork the bottle, shake and leave for two days. Wash an orange. Cut a long strip of the zest. Put this in the bottle containing the vodka and spices, and leave for another 24 hours before straining the vodka and serving it, well-chilled, at the Christmas table.

Crayfish Vodka
70 cl

1 BOTTLE (70 CL) OF VODKA
3 TBSPS ANISEED
1 1/2 TBSPS FENNEL SEEDS
1/2 TBSP. CARAWAY SEED

Procedure:
Put 3 tbsps aniseed, 1 1/2 tbsps fennel seeds and 1/2 tbsp. caraway seed into a litre bottle. Pour on the contents of a 70 cl bottle of vodka, screw the cap on and leave to stand at room temperature for 2 days, followed by 3 to 5 days in the fridge, then strain the vodka and serve it, well-chilled, to go with the crayfish.

Polka Shot
70 cl

1 BOTTLE (70 CL) OF VODKA
1-2 BAGS OF STRIPED CANDY "POLKAGRISKARAMELLER"

Procedure:
Crush the sweets and pour the bits into the bottle.

Elderflower drink
1 glass

2 TBSPS CONCENTRATED ELDERFLOWER JUICE "FLÄDERSAFT"
1 1/2 DL CARBONATED MINERAL WATER
2 CL VODKA
1 SLICE OF LEMON
ICE

Or
2 TBSPS CONCENTRATED ELDERFLOWER JUICE "FLÄDERSAFT"
1 1/2 SPARKLING WHITE WINE
1 SLICE OF LEMON

Wolf's Paw
1 glass

VODKA
CONCENTRATED LINGONBERRY JUICE "LINGONSAFT"
CARBONATED MINERAL WATER

Procedure:
Mix 2 cl vodka, 2 tbsps concentrated lingonberry juice
and 1 1/2 dl mineral water per glass. Serve on the rocks.

A real Swedish coffee party is a feast for the eye – a work of art and no time for hurrying. With all respect for the coffee and home baking, the social side of the occasion is no less important.

Coffee party

The Swedes are great coffee-drinkers. From late 17th century beginnings, they have developed a whole culture of the coffee table.

In addition to the coffee itself, a coffee party also includes a variety of cakes and pastries. The cinnamon bun is a classic, but Swedish ginger snaps and biscuits are also very much a part of the scene.

Coffee, of course, can mean different things to different people. For those who feel that it needs perking up a bit, a drop of Swedish vodka can do the trick, one classic recipe being to put a coin on the bottom of the cup, pour on coffee till the coin disappears, add Swedish vodka till it comes back into view, and then top up with coffee again. "Out of the strong came forth sweetness," as it were.

There can be no children's party without candy. Lots of candy! Put it in bowls, decorate the cake with it, make it prizes for the sack race or put it in bags to take home. Or, better still, all these things at once. And if the sweets run out, there is always cakes and biscuits, with a glass of cold squash to go with them.

Children's party

Children make ideal guests at table – keen, uninhibited and ever-hungry. What better inspiration could a home cook wish for?

In Sweden, like the rest of the world, the children themselves decide the menu, and often this results in variants on the theme of traditional Swedish home fare. Easy to make, with flavours congenial to most kiddy-palates. Serve with elderflower or lingonberry squash. And candy, of course. Tons of it. From those wonderfully leathery "foam cars" (distant relatives of jelly babies) to good Swedish chocolate. So let the kids in and your hair down!

This is what can happen when the child within you is let loose. Toothpicks have turned what began as a cabbage into an exciting new creation bedecked with meatballs and cubes of cheese. The same can be done with vegetables. The pancake gâteau is another guaranteed winner. You'll find both pancake mix and jam in the shop.

Pancake gâteau
Serves 5-6

1 PKT PANCAKE MIX "PANNKAKSMIX"
3 DL WHIPPING CREAM
BLUEBERRY AND RASPBERRY JAM "DROTTNINGSYLT"

Procedure:
Make the pancakes as instructed on the packet. Whip the cream. Make alternate layers of pancakes, whipped cream and jam. Garnish with a knob of cream and more jam.

List of recipes

Small dishes

Salmon recipes